MARY'S LAMB

Copyright 2020 by Richard I. Gold

All rights reserved. No part of this book may be reproduced or transmitted in any form or by any means, electronic or mechanical, including photocopying, or recording, or by any information storage and retrieval system without written permission from publisher or author. The only exception is brief quotations for review.

The information address

J2B Publishing LLC
4251 Columbia Park Road
Pomfret, MD 20657
www.J2BLLC.com
GladToDoIt@gmail.con

This book is set in Garamond
Cover by: Penelope Gold/Richard Gold

ISBN:978-1-9488747-81-3

MARY'S LAMB

Richard I. Gold
J2B Publishing

Also by Richard I. Gold

Psalms of Praise
Many Do Not Know My Jesus
The Wishing Tree
I Bless You God
Mary's Lamb
Work is a 4-Letter Word
Remember the Good Times
God's Love-Easter Poems
Life us a Trip
Free Advice
Christmas Trees and Mistletoe
Cost of the Cross
The Tree of Salvation
The Wall
So much to Accomplish
My Ghost
Sayings for the Believer
God's Agenda

Dedication

My thanks for the support of my Wife, Penney Gold, who helped in the initial editing of this work.

TABLE OF CONTENTS

INTRODUCTION
INSPIRATION
MARY'S LAMB 1
MARY HAD A LITTLE LAMB 2
MARY'S CHILD..3
MARY'S HOLY LAMB...4
AS THE DAYS GROW COLD 6
THE NIGHT 9
ON A NIGHT LONG AGO 10
THE STAR 12
JESUS, BABY IN A MANGER 14
WHEN WE THINK OF CHRISTMAS 15
BUT GOD 16
WHEN I WAS VERY YOUNG 18
JESUS CHRIST BORN TODAY 19
JESUS CHRIST CAME.. 20
CHRISTMAS IS A TIME OF LOVE 22
THE HOLY LAMB OF MARY 23
THE SCHEDULE OF GOD 24
JESUS WAS BORN IN A DISTANT LAND 25
JESUS CHRIST WAS BORN ON EARTH 26
WHAT IS CHRISTMAS?... 27
CHRISTMAS IS COMING.. 28
TO ALL WE WISH 30
WINTER IS HERE 31
THE HOLIDAY SEASON.. 32
CHRISTMAS IS A TIME OF YEAR........................ 33
CHRISTMAS COMES EACH YEAR 34
CHRISTMAS IS OUR HOLY TIME 36
JOY TO THE WORLD.. 37

AWAY IN THE MANGER	38
THE COMING OF THE BOSS	40
IT IS THE SEASON	44
THE HOPE	45
GOD CHOSE TO WORK WITH MEN	46
IT WAS A TIME OF TURMOIL	48
THE SON OF GOD CAME	50
FOR THE LIGHT OF THE LORD	51
THE SON OF GOD	52
SON OF MAN, SON OF GOD	54
TO GOD BE THE GLORY	56
GOD AND JESUS ARE ONE	57
TO KNOW GOD	58
TO KNOW CHRIST	60
HOLY SPIRIT	62
I BLESS YOU GOD	63
DAYS LONG AGO	64
CHRIST CAME TO US	66
REMEMBER	67
GOD'S CHILDREN	68
JESUS CHRIST, JESUS CHRIST	69
JESUS	70
GOD SENT	72
BY THE LOVE OF GOD	74
THE HOLY PRAISE	75
GOD OF HEAVEN	76
GOD LOVED US	77
THEN JESUS CAME IN	78
WHEN CHRIST WAS BORN	79
SNOW	80
SNOWFLAKES ON THE TREES	81
NEW SNOW	82

WHAT CHRISTMAS MEANS	83
SNOW FLAKES AND FROSTY BREATH	84
THAT TIME OF YEAR	85
A TIME OF LOVE	86
THE WORLD IS FULL OF FUN	87
END OF YEAR	88
THE OFFICE PARTY	90
WHEN I WAS SMALL	91
THE SEASON OF GOOD CHEER	92
CHRISTMAS IS THAT TIME	93
THE DAYS OF SUMMER	94
THE COLD WIND	95
ANOTHER DAY, ANOTHER YEAR	96
THE SEASON IS COMING	97
DAYS GROW SHORT	98
ON EASTER	99
THE END OF THE YEAR	100
WE HOPE THIS YEAR	102
AS THE NEW DAY DAWNS	103
THE HOPES	104
LIFE IS A TRIP	105
YEAR IN, YEAR OUT	106
A NEW DAY DAWNS	107
ANOTHER YEAR	108
YEAR OF LOVE	109
ROAD OF LIFE	110
TO ALL WE WISH	111
CHRISTMAS IS THE TIME OF YEAR	112
THE END OF THE WORLD	113
WHEN IN THE COURSE	114
GIVE THANKS	115
WHO IS GOD?	116

MEASURING TIME	117
THERE IS ONE WAY	118
THE SEARCH	120
THE SPECIAL DAY	122
THE DAYS GROW SHORT	123
WINTER GOLF	124
HOME WITH FRIENDS	126
CHRISTMAS HOLIDAY	127
THE DAYS OF CHRISTMAS	128
ABOUT THE AUTHOR	129

INTRODUCTION

Most people are familiar with the poem MARY HAD A LITTLE LAMB.

Mary had a little lamb
Its fleece was white as snow
And everywhere that Mary went
The lamb was sure to go

The poem as written is about a girl named Mary who took her pet lamb to school. However, this can also be interpreted to help us learn about Mary the mother of Jesus and His relationship to her. In this poem, Jesus is the Lamb of God and it can be used to teach children and us about the Holy Family.

INSPIRATION

The author's mother was a poet all her life, producing numerous poems and plays. She inspired the author to begin writing poems later in life. These poems were inspired by the Christmas season, the end of the year and winter in general which has a very rich source of inspiration. Thus, many of the poems are related to the season, and to the way we celebrate the birth and life of Christ. Some poems also apply to the Christian experience through the total life of Christ. Also included are secular Christmas poems and seasonal (winter) poems which reflect the time of year.

NOTE: At some places the term "men" is used in the generic sense to denote the whole human race, not just men. This term is retained because it fits into the meter of the poem. In some of the poems the word "One" is capitalized, because it refers to Jesus. And the word "Way" is sometimes capitalized when used as the original designation for the Christian Life.

MARY'S LAMB

Mary's Lamb, Lamb of God
Born the first Christmas day
Born a small and helpless Child
Born to tell God's Way

Long ago, in a land faraway
God's Holy Gift was given
The plan of our Holy God
Giving us the way to Heaven

Much has happened since that day
In the world of men
The message of the Holy Gift from God
Has changed not from when it began

So let us truly worship
The One sent from God above
That by His will and by His might
We may receive His eternal love

MARY HAD A LITTLE LAMB

Mary had a little Lamb
A little Lamb had she
So little and precious
What does this mean to me?

Mary lad a little Lamb
The Son of God was He
Died for my sins
That's what it means to me

Mary's Lamb was raise to life anew
Raised by the power of God above
Given to the sons of men
Given by eternal love

Mary had a little Lamb
Born on that special day
Born to make us whole
Born to show us the Way

Mary had a little Lamb
Came to guide us in what we do
Came to show us how to act
Came to make our actions true

MARY'S CHILD

Because God loved mankind so
He sent us Mary's Child
To show us the Way to live
The Way peaceful and mild

Mary's Child was born that night
Into the world of men
It was His holy task
To show us how to begin

Mary's Child came to the world of men
Came by human birth
To show us the way to God
To show us our heavenly worth

Mary's Child, Mary's Child
It was such a beginning
By God's Will He taught
Forever until life's ending

MARY'S HOLY LAMB

Mary's Holy Lamb born so long ago
Born the Son of God
Born the Son of Man
Born to guide us as through life we trod

We celebrate the Lamb of God
Born to humankind
That by the love of God
Heaven we may find

Thankful, we should forever be
As on the path of life we trod
That in the now and in the end
Our path will lead to the feet of God

Mary's Holy Lamb is full of love
For the race of men
He live upon this earth
Where we're often overcome by sin

Mary's Lamb came to earth
Born on Christmas day
By the hand of God
Came to wash our sins away

Lived so long ago
Lived among the children of men
Walk upon the earth
Showed us forgiveness of sin

Remember His birth and life
Remember all He gave
A Way to live upon the earth
To take us to Heaven from the grave

Let not the way we would take
Be the road we follow
Else when we reach the end of life
We will find the destination hollow

No person may get to Heaven
By following their nose
But it is the Way of the Lamb
That teaches how eternity goes

AS THE DAYS GROW COLD

As the days grow cold
The love of God shows us
He sent His only Son
In Him we must ever trust

On the first Christmas day
People did not know the score
They wished for all that is
Then they wished for even more

On that day there was no tree
No lights or tinsel then
Only the precious Gift
That God above did send

He sent to all humankind
From the depth of His Love
The most He had ever sent
From His throne above

So dark the first night
So quiet the children of men
When God acted with love and power
A new age to begin

The message of that day
Resounds down through all ages
To the children of men today
The love told by the sages

The first Christmas night
Started a chain of events
That a Holy Revelation
Was to our hearts sent

There were few who knew
That first Christmas night
What a fateful thing happened
That would end in eternal Light

We look back to that night
The beginning of all things good
Still shows us today
In our hearts God's love could

There is no other thing
No other Way given to men
To live and be right with God
That we must follow to the end

Let us know the truth
Given that first Christmas day
We can come to know
We must follow His Way

The Way of God above
The birth of His Only Son
Set in motion events
Eternity has begun

Eternal life that God doth give
Began that first Christmas day
For it was the plan of God
That the Babe would for our sins pay

THE NIGHT

Long ago in a distant land
A small Child was born
Sent by Heaven's will
Into the world forlorn

It was Mary's Child born that night
Sent by God's Holy power
To be our key to Heaven above
So that we may live there forever

There is much we can never know
Why God chose to send His Son
That we may be made right with Him
When our Spiritual life has begun

The message of that Little Life
Has echoed in the hearts of men
That when we seek to know the Way to God
He shows us how we can begin

ON A NIGHT LONG AGO

On a night long ago
To some poor shepherds in the field
There shown a bright light
Fear in them was filled

An angel came out of the night
To tell them the good news
It had not happened before
The angel told them true

"Be not afraid." the angel said
"For unto you this day
God's promise has been given
To show you the way"

"There is a small Baby born
The hope of all mankind
Go to the city of Bethlehem
There, the Baby you will find"

Then they went
With hope, they did rejoice
They told all who heard
Of the heavenly voice

The mother and child
Who in a manger lay
The promise of God
Given that fateful day

Returning to their field
They did not know what to say
For who would believe them
Or what they saw that day

But to the mother
Their report did enthrall
For it was a message of hope
To the people all

The message to us today
Is the same as it was then
We can but believe the truth
That shows us how to begin

THE STAR

In the sky one night
Wise men saw a new star
They realized it was special
The promise in a land so far

The promise was given by God
To the children of men
Given to those of old
That a new age was about to begin

This was a signal
To those learned in the sky
They knew that it was time to search
The new age began now, that's why

They traveled to the distant land
To tell the king of the Jews
A new king was born
Perhaps he would laud the news

But the king did not think this good
Another to seek his throne
He would kill the upstart
But did not let this be known

The wise men went to search
For the newfound King
But they did not know the end of it
Or that the angels would sing

The wise men found the Child
Whom they worshiped with treasures and gold
To show that they honored Him
Then left the evil king untold

So now we worship Him
The Babe grown to be a Man
With more than earthly treasures
In every way we can

Let us know the Way to worship
Let us give our very self in love
To worship with the angels of God
To honor that Babe above

JESUS, BABY IN A MANGER

Jesus, Baby in a manger
So gentle and so mild
Born so long ago
Lived with love, no guile

Jesus, Boy in the land
Grew from Baby to Man
Told the Word of God
For life's race He ran

Jesus, Man in the world
Walked a land so far away
Taught us how to live
So our sin debt He would pay

Jesus, Man of pain and sorrow
Lived and died so far away
But that is not the end of it
We know the truth of that day

Jesus, victorious and strong
Rose by God's power from death to life
Now sits at God's right hand
Saves us from eternal strife

WHEN WE THINK OF CHRISTMAS

When we think of Christmas
Oft we think of things
Parties and songs
Of silver bells that ring

Remember the day of Christmas
The joy it can bring
For we celebrate the birthday
Of Jesus, our Lord and King

In time we forget
The gifts under the tree
But we can never forget
The gift from Heaven, so free

God's gift to all humankind
Saved us from the grave
We should never forget
The joy He gave

BUT GOD

The days grow cold
The nights grow long
It sometimes seems
The world is full of wrong

But God

Many years ago
In a land far away
A small Baby was born
On that fateful day

But God

There was no celebration
In the world of men
But that Baby set the pace
For a new world to begin

But God

We must follow His teaching
Of faith and of love
To be like our Heavenly Father
Who guides us from above

But God

We work the works of men
We try to do our best
But without God's guidance
Our work will turn to dust

But God

God gave His only Son
To come and teach us how
To know right from wrong
To know it here and now

But God

God who loves mankind
He wishes for us the best
Can guide our hands and thoughts
So we may be called blessed

WHEN I WAS VERY YOUNG

When I was very young
Christmas was a time of joys
With lots of good food
Of family and lots of toys

As I became a little older
I learned there is more to life
I learned the secret of believing
There is more to Christmas than receiving

I learned the reason
We have love and good cheer
Was not what we get
But that the Son of God was here

Then I grew to know His love
Learn what He would want
For us to love each other
And aid those who don't

So we must be unto others
A source of love and care
This is how we will be judged
In Heaven when we get there

JESUS CHRIST BORN TODAY

(To the tune of "Do you know the Muffin Man?")

Jesus Christ was born today
Was born today
Was born today
Jesus Christ was born today
To teach us God's Holy Way

Jesus Christ came down to earth
Came down to earth
Came down to earth
Jesus Christ came down to earth
To give us the Second Birth

Jesus Christ is in Heaven now
In Heaven now
In Heaven now
Jesus Christ is in Heaven now
God will forgive our sins, that's how

JESUS CHRIST CAME

Jesus Christ came to earth
Came to show us the Second Birth
Born the Son of Man
Born in a manger

Lived with those who knew Him best
Lived to save all the rest
They didn't know who He was
So they might be God's Blest

Taught us how to pray
Taught us what we should say
Taught us how we should live
Taught us God's Holy Way

Died upon a Roman cross
Died for all to save
Few knew the loss
By the life He gave

God raised Him from the grave
Rose to God on high
By this act He might save
Lives in Heaven beyond the sky

Jesus Christ, the Son of God
Born to save us to New Life
Born to give us love and life
Came to save us from the strife

CHRISTMAS IS A TIME OF LOVE

Christmas is a time of love
A time to forgive
For God sent His only Son
To teach us how to live

We suffer many wrongs
Others to us have done
How can we forgive?
How can forgiveness be begun?

But our sins against God
Are much, much the greater
If He could forgive us at all
He has love because He is our maker

"Forgive them" were the words of Christ
As He hung upon that tree
If He could forgive His tormenters
Surely, I can forgive thee

THE HOLY LAMB OF MARY

Mary had a Holy Lamb
The Son of God was He
By His life and by His death
That His Salvation we might see

The Holy Lamb of Mary
A Lamb of God on High
He came so long ago
That God's Love may draw nigh

The Holy Lamb of Mary
Much it means to me
God raised him from the dead
Ere He hung upon a tree

Mary had a Holy Lamb
This is what we must see
For by His message bold
We can live through all eternity

THE SCHEDULE OF GOD

In the schedule of God
Mary had a Loving Lamb
A Loving Lamb had she
Lived so long ago
What does this mean to me?

The Loving Lamb of Mary
The Son of God is He
Came and lived upon earth
What does this mean to me?

God's Loving Lamb came by Mary
Lived and died upon a tree
Raised by God to life anew
Everlasting life has He

Mary had a loving Lamb
Salvation given so free
So I might have eternal life
That's what it means to me

JESUS WAS BORN IN A DISTANT LAND

Jesus was born in a distant land
Our sin debt for to pay
Came to tell us of God
Came to teach us God's Holy Way

Jesus was born on that special day
Customs different from us now
Sent to the children of men
To teach us Heaven's "how"

The thoughts of man have not changed
From that time long ago
We must have salvation
So we can through the gates of Heaven go

Jesus was born at a distant time
People did different from what they now do
We have changed in who we are
But His teachings still are true

JESUS CHRIST WAS BORN ON EARTH

Jesus Christ was born on earth
Amen, amen
Born to give us Second Birth
Amen, amen
Lived so long ago
Amen, amen
Lived so God we may know
Amen, amen

Taught us how we should give
Amen, amen
Taught us how we must live
Amen, amen
There is much of God men may know
Amen, amen
No other way we may go
Amen, amen

No other way to Heaven on High
Amen, amen
When to eternity we draw nigh
Amen, amen
We must follow His Way
Amen, amen
It is our duty to try
Amen, amen

WHAT IS CHRISTMAS?

What is Christmas?
What is that day?
Santa Claus and presents
Baby Jesus in the hay

Memories of Christmas past
Of love and peace and joy
Christmas trees and presents
Is that my toy?

Christmas has many memories
Pleasant memories of love
That the Son of God
Was sent to us from above

Christmas is and always was
A celebration of a time of love
When all may be forgiven
By the Will of Him in Heaven above

CHRISTMAS IS COMING

Christmas is coming
This time of year
For presents and parties
Santa and reindeer

Giving of presents
Is such a delight
Shopping in the malls
Is such a fight

Parties are fun
Full of good cheer
Come January
Dieting is here

Santa gives joyful delight
His reindeer are so nice
When we see all the tinsel
It leaves us on ice

Parties and presents
Shopping grows old
Leaves me exhausted
Of body and soul

Things we get and give
Are not the only reason
We celebrate
This joyous season

For the One born of old
Born so we may know
We have a Way of life
There is one Holy Way we must go

The world was one of desire
When men had gone astray
The message sent from God
There is but one Holy Way

The One Who was born
Gave meaning to this day
That He had God's message
He taught us how to pray

So we should rejoice
That now we know the truth
To live as we must in life
Live according to God's Sooth

TO ALL WE WISH

To all we wish a happy holiday
To your kind and kin
May this season glow
We wish a good New Year to begin

In this world of toil and sin
There is much we cannot know
But to give to others good
As through the year we go

Enjoy life as it comes
The bad and the good
It is our troubles
That makes us be as we should

Have a holy season
From Heaven above
Let us know the truth
Of fellowship and love

WINTER IS HERE

Winter is here
With ice and snow
When the blizzard comes
There's no place to go

But not all is bad
When ere we stay home
This is the time of year
When our heart is warm

Warm house and warm home
Makes a warm heart
For the ones we love
We are so glad to do our part

For we celebrate
Christmas is here
It is our Savior's birth
So let us have good cheer

THE HOLIDAY SEASON

The holidays are a special time
Thanksgiving, Christmas and New Year
It makes us be our best
With love and good cheer

We should look out for others
And try to help them so
When we look only to ourselves
The spirit of the season will go

Within the heart of men
Is a burning fire we note
That when we look to others
It will give others hope

So remember to reason
For the love and good cheer
We celebrate our Savior's birth
Who walked and taught us here

CHRISTMAS IS A TIME OF YEAR

Christmas is a time of year
When even enemies have good cheer
The malls are open with anticipation great
That shoppers will come - just can't wait

Late night parties and Holy Rite
Come every day, every night
Wishing all that you see
That you'll be as happy as me

No time to wait
No time to dally
For when it's all over
Our bills we will tally

It's Santa and reindeer
It's Christ in the Church
The season is dear
Leave no one in a lurch

So sing all the songs
Be of good cheer
Right all wrongs
Christmas comes but once a year

CHRISTMAS COMES EACH YEAR

Christmas comes each year
Bringing love, hope and good cheer
For parties and friends so dear
A time to get ready for the New Year

Christmas is made for children
For Santa with good toys
Things under the tree
For all good girls and boys

Come, let us enjoy
Know that despite the fuss
Because Christmas is given
As a present to us

Christmas is the time of year
For presents and old St. Nick
When we give unto others
Watching them receive gives us a kick

For those who are all alone
For those who have no one
This time of year is very hard
Makes them wish they were gone

But for those who are with them
Who give themselves to others
Live with a spirit of warmth and love
Treat the lonely ones like brothers

CHRISTMAS IS OUR HOLY TIME

Christmas is our holy time
For us to have love, joy and good cheer
It is both beginning and end
Of the time so dear

He came to show us love
And the glorious Way
To live with each other
And know what to say

Try, try to remember the reason
We celebrate this time of year
It is a joyous remembrance
That Heaven came down the be here

When I see the Christmas tree
And the presents there for me
I will try to remember He
He who came to set me free

JOY TO THE WORLD

Joy to the world
Joy we can forever sing
Praise we give
Praise we bring

Sing songs of joy
Sing songs of praise
To the highest King
All the Holy Days

There is non-other
He is the only One
Who gave Himself
Who is salvation's Son

Praise be to our Maker
Praise be for His Might
Give glory to our Maker
Both by day and by night

AWAY IN THE MANGER

Away in the manger
Away from our sight
The Son of God was born
That holy night

The angels announced
The blessed event
So that all people
Could know God's intent

But He was rejected
By men then as now
For to worship the Son of God
They did not know how

They thought He was a man
Just like you and me
Because of the rejection
They hung him on a tree

But God fooled them
With power divine
He raised Him to life anew
Life like yours and mine

In His resurrection we trust
In His teachings we live
And find salvation
The gift only He can give

THE COMING OF THE BOSS

In a country long ago
In a world we can imagine but never know
The world was ruled by a ruthless power
Who took what they would
All others were made to cower

At the edge of their empire
In a small country so weak
Ruled a ruthless king
His subjects to him obedience did bring

There was a poor girl
Who was good in every way
While she was living her life
An angel came to say

"You have found favor with God
You will forever the world bless
For you will have a Holy Son"
This put her in a state of distress

"How can this be?
I have never had a man?"
But the angel assured her
"With God all things are possible"

"You have never had the passion
That a man can bring
But the Holy Union
Will cause angels to sing"

So it was with this maid
So it will be with all mankind
The message that was brought
Was what men of God did find

Then the foreign power
That ordered people what to do
Made her and her husband
To Bethlehem go

There a Small Baby was born
In a feeding trough He was placed
This showed the humility of His birth
God's Eternal Grace

Then to poor shepherds
Living in a field
Angels came to tell the Good News
Their hearts were thrilled

After the angels left
They went to see
What this miracle was
What it could ever be

They came to see the Baby
Lying in a manger
To Mary and Joseph they told
The heavenly vision seemed stranger

Then, later from the east
Came learned men
First to Jerusalem
To ask where their search should begin

They were told to go to Bethlehem
Where the scriptures said the Christ would be born
It was the city of David, the King
They came and found the One on the holy morn

Great gifts they brought
Myrrh, frankincense and gold
They were looking for a king
Their literature had foretold

Then they departed
Did not see the brutal king
Joseph and Mary left for Egypt
So that in the future we may sing

That was long ago
In a world different from the one I know
But the message that to us it doth bring
Makes my very soul sing

IT IS THE SEASON

It is the season
It is the reason
It is the day and night
It is the point of Light

Christmas is the season
For eating, parties and fun
It would be better
If I did not have to run

For those who have seen the Light
Who worship as do I
Christmas has a reason
The answer to the question "Why"

The day of Christmas
Is a celebration of Light
And if we have faith
It is a celebration of the Right

THE HOPE

To this world of toil and sin
To those without hope at all
Was born a small Child
Who came to save us from the fall

Did the world know the gift?
Did they celebrate?
It was a clueless world
Filled with sin and hate

But He gave to us hope
Of life eternal and new
That by what He did and what He taught
Was then and now eternally true

The hope the Child brought
Was one for all the ages
A hope that is known to all
Understood by the sages

So let us know this hope
That we may forever be
When at the feet of God
His hope, His power we may see

GOD CHOSE TO WORK WITH MEN

In a time a long ago
In a land far away
God chose to work with men
To show to us His Holy Way

To a poor girl
Came the power of God
To make a Man Child
To give all people the nod

It was the purpose of this Man Child
To tell of God's truth and love
That forever we may know
The Holy Message from above

The poor girl was Mary
She guided the Man Child in youth
Helped Him to know what He should do
As He came to realize the truth

The birth of the Man Child
Was not the end of it all
For when He became a Man
What he taught saved us from the fall

It is with power and love
That God works His Holy Will
And gives to all mankind
The opportunity to pay sin's bill

IT WAS A TIME OF TURMOIL

It was a time of turmoil
The world was in the grip
The Romans ruled with fear
With the sword and the whip

At the edge of the world
In a country far away
A small Baby was born
On one fateful day

No one took notice
Not the Romans, nor their king
For to the Romans
It did not mean a thing

But when He grew to Manhood
New hope He did bring
To the hopeless and the slaves
His praises they did sing

Today that Babe so small and frail
Has a revolution brought
By His life and by His death
And by God's Word He taught

Hope of the hopeless
Salvation for all mankind
Will bring us to Heaven
And Satan - He will bind

THE SON OF GOD CAME

The Son of God came
God's Holy Will to show
He taught and lived and died
God's Way for us to know

He was killed by evil men
They hung Him upon a tree
It seemed to be the end
What does this mean to me?

By God's power and by God's will
Jesus was raised from the grave
That by God's Word and by God's Hand
All mankind may be saved

There is but one Way, one Path
By which we must be saved
That in God's wisdom and by His will
We'll live beyond the grave

So praise the Lord
Praise His Holy Name
For throughout all eternity
He is from age to age the same

FOR THE LIGHT OF THE LORD

For the light of the Lord
For the glory of His love
For sending us His Son
We give thanks to the One above

There are many things
For which we should rejoice
So we lift our hearts and hands
Sing with heavenly voice

Let us praise the Lord
Praise His Holy Name
For He showed His love and mercy
From age to age the same

Do not let the sun go down
Before you sing God's praise
For He gave His Holy One
To be with us all our days

THE SON OF GOD

The Son of God
Who lived on this earth
Came to mankind
Came by human birth

As He lived with us
He taught and healed
So that our souls may be made whole
Our salvation sealed

Then he died upon a cross
He suffered many things
That by His death
Sin forgiveness brings

God raised Him to life again
Raised Him from the grave
Showed Himself to His disciples
New hope He gave

Now He lives with God
He lives forever there
To be our High Priest
To intercede for our every care

After He came to His followers
He showed He is the risen Lord
He went to Heaven on high
Left us with His Word

Someday He is coming back
Evil ones to judge
The glorious day of God will come
The everlasting begun

For those who are not faithful
Who do not follow in the Way
Will to torment go
There forever to stay

For those who are faithful
Great reward He will bring
Praises to God forever
The faithful will sing

SON OF MAN, SON OF GOD

Son of Man, Son of God
Came to the earth
To show us the Way to live
So we may have the Second Birth

A long time ago He walked among men
He told the path of life
Was thought to be a Prophet
Showed us the end of strife

When He was killed upon a cross
God showed that He is special
God raised Him from the dead
The miracle of all miracles

Now we must follow in His Way
To love and forgive other men
To be in all ways like Him
Although we might not know how to begin

We begin to follow His Way
To live according to God's will
Worship our Lord and King
His commandments to fulfill

In order to be in the Kingdom
The Kingdom of God
We must accept His Holy Writ
Before we are beneath the sod

TO GOD BE THE GLORY

To God be the glory
Great things He has done
He gave us salvation
He sent us His Son

Worship Him in gladness
Worship Him in truth
Give of your substance
Give of the strength of your youth

Know that God is truth
Know that God is Love
Who loves and cares for us
From Heaven above

Praise Him in all things
Praise Him in every way
To Him be the glory
To serve Him every day

GOD AND JESUS ARE ONE

For many years we have heard of God
Who loves us over all
He is the One Who sent His Son
To save us from the fall

Jesus came to save every person
From the Evil One
For those who do not know
Jesus is the Christ, God's only Son

But Jesus had the spirit of God
Within His very Soul
It filled his very being
Filled every part that made Him whole

Jesus was also a man
Tempted like us in every way
God guided His every action
Taught Jesus what to say

We worship God as our Heavenly Father
We pray through Jesus Christ, His Son
But we must remember when we seek Jesus
That God and Jesus are one

TO KNOW GOD

The world is filled with many things
Some things we can know
We learn about most of these
As through life we go

There are other things
Beyond what we can comprehend
Of which we can never learn
If we did, wrong understanding would descend

There are things beyond our knowledge
Beyond the understanding of man
Things we cannot know in this life
As numerous as a beach's sand

We cannot see the face of God
We cannot know His awesome power
Above the history of all people
His presence doth tower

We can know some of His will
For it is that desires He
How to worship Him
His holiness our mind's eye to see

It is His will that we help
Those with less than we have
The widows and the orphans
To the destitute give

Although we cannot see God's face
Although no whisper in our ear
We can know the will of God
Worship Him in reverence and in fear

TO KNOW CHRIST

As we go through life
Many things are to us made known
What we do and where we go
And where we make our home

But there are eternal things
Things known beyond the grave
The One Who came from Heaven above
All mankind to save

To know this One as our own
To follow in His Way
Will, for us to save
And not in eternity have to pay

To know Christ in all His glory
Is to follow what He taught
So that, as through life we go
We can live as we ought

There is no middle way
Where we can be in and out
We follow or we don't
That is that, the eternal shout

So follow the will of God
Know that Jesus is our Lord
We may suffer here on earth
But we shall reap the Holy reward

HOLY SPIRIT

God is a spirit
At work in the world
The power of God is here
All around us it doth swirl

The Spirit of God is our strength
The Spirit, Holy we call
It gives strength to the Christian
As through life we roll

Do not grieve the Spirit
By what we say or do
For the Spirit doth judge
By God's standard that's true

But the Spirit does comfort
As Jesus promised long ago
Despite the trials we face
As through life we go

What does this mean?
What are we to do?
By this we can know God's Will
What is holy, just and true

I BLESS YOU GOD

I bless You God for nature's works
I bless You God for many things
I bless You God for the works of man
For what nature brings

But more than the works of man
More than nature's works
It is God's Holy Love
That leads to Heaven's ramparts

A parade of things given
Are blessings that God does make
For we receive many things
From God for His Holy Sake

Give prayers of thanksgiving
To bless His Holy One
For in His love and in His power
He gave us salvation's Son

DAYS LONG AGO

Days long ago
God sent His Only Son
That we may find Heaven
With teachings from the One

God projected Himself
Into the world of men
So that we must live the Way
The New Covenant to begin

But God is in everything
The Holy Spirit and the Word
That we may know the truth
As through life we are hurled

God is the only One
Who has shown His Way by His Son
Has given us the Holy Path
That our life and soul must run

Do not greave the Spirit
Do not use the holy for personal gain
For when at last we are judged
The judgement shall be plain

No man has seen our Holy God
But only the Son
Who has given us the Way
That by His power Heaven we may have won

CHRIST CAME TO US

Christ came to us long ago
He lived so God we may know
The love of God within our soul
Will guide us protect us, to make us whole

We need His love for our daily life
That with His power we may be
God's Children forevermore
After death Heaven we will see

Now love God with all your heart
Work on earth to do your part
That as God's Children we live our life
And serve for eternity we strive

There is much we may never know
Things in Heaven and things below
For much is the province of God
By faith we may hope to know

By God's Holy Hand
By God's Holy Will
We must walk by faith
Let our souls be still

REMEMBER

Long ago lived our Lord
Who came and loved and taught
The Way we must live
Not by the Devil's snares get caught

He came to save all mankind
By His life and by His death
He was raised from the dead
By God's Holy Breath

We must remember His life
We must remember His love
For His life and His love
Came to us from above

Remember all He taught
From birth until the end
For as we remember the love He gave
By which our new life can begin

GOD'S CHILDREN

Christians are God's Children
Children of the Most High
When in love He calls
Our soul will draw nigh

To be a Child of God is good
But what does it mean
Is it a holy bank account?
Or is it something else unseen

How can Christians be God's Children?
Given by the Hand Most High
Born of the Spirit
To God's will draw nigh

To be the Child of God
Is to be as the Most High
For we are to be like Him
Who calls us to draw nigh

JESUS CHRIST, JESUS CHRIST

Jesus Christ, Jesus Christ,
God's only begotten Son
Came to save us from our sins
Like Him there has been no one

Jesus Christ, Jesus Christ,
Our Savior and our Lord
Taught us how to live
Taught us by His Holy Word

Jesus Christ, Jesus Christ,
Walked upon the earth
Lived and died for our sins
To give us the Second Birth

Jesus Christ, Jesus Christ,
The one, the only one
God raised Him from the dead
God's only begotten Son

JESUS

The world was waiting
For what, it did not know
So God in His love did send
His only Son to help us grow

To be born of a woman
Is common to all
But if we depend upon ourselves
We are headed for the fall

God's Son showed us how
To be of the Spirit born
So from this perverse world
Our spirits may be forever torn

The end of life is the all
That to Heaven we may go
So that at God's feet
We may forever grow

But in this life before the grave
Is where we now must live
Show those about us the Way
That God's Son did give

Live as God would have us live
Worship Him as our Lord
For He has loved our world
Has given us His Holy Word

GOD SENT

God
God sent
God sent His
God sent His only
God sent His only Son

To save
To save me
To save me from
To save me from my sins

That
That I
That I might
That I might have
That I might have eternal
That I might have eternal life

I
I must
I must believe
I must believe in
I must believe in Him
I must believe in Him and follow
I must believe in Him and follow Him

I
I must
I must follow
I must follow His
I must follow His teachings
I must follow His teachings if
I must follow His teachings if I
I must follow His teachings if I would
I must follow His teachings if I would go to Heaven

BY THE LOVE OF GOD

By the love of God
He sent His only Son
To live among us
A human race to run

By the love of God
His Son did die
Crucified upon a tree
Salvation is the reason why

By the love of God
His Son He rose to life anew
To make for us salvation
Both possible and true

By the life of God's Son
We know how to live
By the resurrection of God's Son
Salvation He did give

THE HOLY PRAISE

Give to God the Holy Praise
For He is ancient of days
For we have been blessed
To Him we give blessings and praise

God sent His Son
To save us from sin
That when we have passed over
It will be the victory we win

Our salvation He gave
Through death on a cross
That victory came
From what seemed a loss

Praise is all we can give
To Him who is on High
That by His Holy Will
To Him we may draw nigh

GOD OF HEAVEN

God of Heaven
God of earth
Sent His only Son
So we may have the Second Birth

God of earth
God of Heaven
The way of Eternal Life
His Word He's given

God of you
God of me
God sent His only Son
From sin to set us free

God of me
God of you
God gave me the way
That is holy and true

GOD LOVED US

God loved us so much
He sent His only Son
To teach us how to live
To teach us how salvation had begun

In His life and in His death
Our model He is to be
That in the end of life
Our God we may see

The love of God is Holy
The love of God is pure
So that my soul may be made holy
My eternal live sure

We must follow in His steps
In all we say and do
That when our life is over
He will judge us good and true

THEN JESUS CAME IN

Life was an eternal drag
Of ill from day to day
There was no hope for tomorrow
We could not see the Way

Then Jesus came in

Jesus arrested my doubts and sin
He told me how
My blessings run over
I'm better now

Lord, I hold You Holy
In all I know
For I am in holy awe
I reap what I sow

Now my life is better
For by Your Holy Hand
You have given me hope
Given by the Holy Man

WHEN CHRIST WAS BORN

When Christ was born
He came to live and taught
About the Second Birth
How to live as we ought

We know now Who He was
Of how He came to save
The will of God He showed
Eternal life, eternal happiness He gave

That through the time of old
And through the time of new
The first can leave some cold
The second can leave others without a clue

Let us know the will of God
By study and by faith we have
That when we are below the sod
We will with God have the hope He gave

SNOW

For those who live in colder clime
Those who have to travel out
There is a word that clogs the mind
Really has great clout

What is that word
It is as every driver does know
The word gives us chills
That word is snow

It clogs the roads
It clogs the walks
It stops the world
All we can do is talk

How do we remove this bane
It takes the breaking back
We shovel it to one side
Exercise we do not lack

But believing the use of nature
Is how we should run
That to remove the snow
We rely on nature's sun

SNOWFLAKES ON THE TREES

Snowflakes in the trees
Sparkle in the sun
Days are short, year is closing
It's race almost run

Comes Christmas time
Of Santa and good cheer
Brings us hope, brings us joy
This time of year

Though we may not like snow
When we go out
It is a time to celebrate
When the holiday happiness mount

Christmas lights and tinsel
All sitting on the tree
Gives a feeling of love
To both you and me

NEW SNOW

A silver moon across the land
A cold wind doth blow
To grandma's house we go
Through the cold, cold snow

With presents piled high
Wrapped with paper and ribbon
Each present from our heart
So part of us is given

So we should be happy
For this time of year
For when the New Year comes
New opportunities are here

Let's go and celebrate
With tinsel and good cheer
Good times and good friends
Christmas brings so near

WHAT CHRISTMAS MEANS

What does Christmas mean to you?
A tale of Christmas past
A time of loving others
A time we wished would last

But time marches on
So it is with us
We grow and learn our way
To do what we must

Remember when we were kids
We could hardly wait for thee
For Christmas morning
What do I get under the tree

Now we are older
Now we remember long ago
That it was the love of others
That made Christmas glow

So go and love others
With a love so pure and true
That when Christmas has come and gone
Your life, your love will endure

SNOW FLAKES AND FROSTY BREATH

Snow flakes and frosty breath
The season of year grows cold
As the end of year approaches
The year grows old

But amid the darkness
Glows as in days of old
A time makes our spirits soar
Our selves grow bold

Yule tide logs and mistletoe
Make our spirits bright
As we prepare for the time
In the dark of night

Let us truly celebrate
For a joyous time of year
So we can both get and give
For those who we truly care

The time goes so fast
For soon the future will be here
With the opportunities and hopes
The special New Year

THAT TIME OF YEAR

The birds have flown south
To find a warmer clime
For those who remain here
It is winter time

Look to the future
Next year is close
With opportunities untold
We will have much to boast

We celebrate with others
To give love and good care
For when the New Year is here
Our hope will be there

There are many good times
This time of year
So let us rejoice
With good cheer

A TIME OF LOVE

Christmas is a time of love
Of laughter and many joys
As kids we liked good food
With our family and lots of toys

As we grew into our prime
Began to give not get
We began to know the time
When we have a greater joy yet

For those who give us gifts
We know what we should do
Write a nice letter to them
Say to them a great big "THANK YOU"

When we give a gift
We ourselves we do give
To make someone happy
It is the best way to live

THE WORLD IS FULL OF FUN

The world is full of fun
Of laughter and good cheer
That sets the world a jar
Makes us glad we're here

As we go through life
We stop to have some fun
We do not always give our self
As we should have begun

We each have our personal life
We keep to ourselves
That we may live with others
Not be left on the shelf

So as we enter Christmas time
Full of presents and good cheer
Let us remember those about us
Help those we hold dear

END OF YEAR

There is nothing like the end of year
To sum up all that we've done
The things we would like to do
The things we have begun

We never have done all we would
But somehow the year has gone
Now comes New Year
With it a new dawn

What will the New Year bring?
What will we be there in?
To be a better person
To be a friend of men

As cold weather comes
We have a chance to sit and think
About the future that we would
The resolutions we will make

The future belongs to us
To all we would do
Our wishes and our hopes
May it be both good and true

So let us share with those we love
Our family and our friends
The New Year to be the way
To make better things begin

THE OFFICE PARTY

Wednesday is the office party
In celebration of Christmas
We all will over eat
Make our diet a mess

We will socialize
With others in the office
Exchange good wishes
With sincerity in our voice

We eat and drink the punch
We wish it could last
When this time of year is over
All will remember the Christmas past

When we finish
Leave the building
We will head for home
Be thankful for our filling

WHEN I WAS SMALL

When I was small
My mother was tall
And Christmas was a time of getting
We were kids all
Having a ball
When we were in this setting

As I grew older
My thoughts became bolder
And Christmas became a time of giving
When the days grow colder
I had to have a way to shoulder
The help for those who need the living

Now I remember days gone by
I think why
The past is ever with me
When looking back
I know the tack
That helps me the truth to see

THE SEASON OF GOOD CHEER

It is the season of good cheer
Of celebration with those so dear
Of candles and all light
Brightens both soul and night

For those who are far away
Our spirit is with you this day
That the soul may truly warm
Keep our spirit from all harm

We are thankful for life and health
For all we will know to give
But let us remember always
Those who are without what we have

Remember those who have less
Help those who are in distress
Our soul will truly glow
As through this joyous season we go

CHRISTMAS IS THAT TIME

Christmas is that time of year
For parties, presents and good cheer
For singing the songs we sing only now
Santa comes down the chimney, but how

Look out on the snow
It makes you glad
You have a warm house
That cannot be bad

Sometimes what we have
Is a blessing we need
Yet for all things
Is what we often plead

Unto others we see
Who have a need
Our hearts go out
With their situation doth plead

So let us open
Our minds and hearts
With a holy concern
We do our part

THE DAYS OF SUMMER

The days of summer are gone
The cold wind doth blow
The north lands are cold
They shall have snow

In the sunny south
Winter is not so bad
It gives but a greeting
Of what the snow birds have had

Those in all places
Can have good cheer
For when Christmas comes
It will be a blessing here

But the holidays are for all
May they bring you good cheer
And all good things
In the coming year

THE COLD WIND

The days become short
A cold wind doth blow
Cooling the body but by Christmas
Within the soul doth glow

It is the season of love
Joy and good cheer
For before we know it
The holidays are here

Go shopping in force
To the stores and malls
Shop till you drop
Listen, the holiday calls

But stop for a moment
For peace of your soul
It'll pay dividends
Keep life on a roll

Enjoy this season with joy
Do not fear
For this season will come again
At this time next year

ANOTHER DAY, ANOTHER YEAR

Another day, another year
Has come and gone its way
We can but remember the good that was
The kind words that people say

Now is the time we have
For life and good cheer
To be with those we love
To be with those we hold dear

As into the future we go
We know not what tomorrow will be
But may it be the best for you
In the New Year, good joy you'll see

So have a happy holiday
So let it be to you
Some kind word or deed
That are good, faithful and true

THE SEASON IS COMING

The season is coming
The season is here
A time for celebration
It is a New Year

As the year changes again
All things become new
Wish you good health
Wealth that's true

When days are cold
The north wind doth blow
May warmest friendships
Be what you know

Keep always warn
In body and soul
For the New Year is coming
The new day will make us whole

DAYS GROW SHORT

Days grow short
It is that time of year
When we look back
With sadness and good cheer

For this year is passing
In much we did succeed
Even when we failed
Our progress it did not impede

For the New Year is coming
Let us look and smile
Let any troubles
Be short and mild

We enter a new age
So have a good New Year
For the future is yours
Good luck and good cheer

ON EASTER

On Easter we remember the death of a Man
Who was born on Christmas Day
He came and taught the love of God
He died for our sins to pay

We remember the way He showed us
To be the Children of God on high
That in this life to live
In eternity we may to God draw nigh

He was killed by evil men
By those who did not know
They could not do the right
Their evil way to show

Then God did a Holy Act
God raised Christ from the dead
That we may find the way
And not have death to dread

So we worship Him in truth
We must follow in His Way
Right actions always
And know what to say

THE END OF THE YEAR

The end of the year
Is not an end but a door
Through which we travel
To new things and more

May this bring you many good things
In this season of hope and joy
So that your hope, your best
You will be able to enjoy

Remember those who have less
For they are many, not few
Who were lost in a storm
Of men and nature, it's true

Do not despair, but always hope
The future is the opportunity, the way
To be remembered by those who linger
Let your actions reflect what you say

For when we are and when we were
Those in need will our memory hold
That we were not self-centered
But were for others bold

We cannot solve all the world's problems
But there is a difference we can make
That we give to others in need
Give more than we take

May this season be a blessing
May you remembered be
A help to those in need
That by your actions a better world they'll see

WE HOPE THIS YEAR

We hope this year has been good
All your wishes have come true
By the by you will be blessed
May your future make all things new

We cannot know the future
It will come when it will
For the bad and for the good
We wait and must be still

The Hew Year is a new beginning
A new path to run
Prepare for the good times
We receive what is to come

May the blessings be to you and yours
That the season will be bold
In the arms of the Almighty
Your true self He will hold

AS THE NEW DAY DAWNS

As the new day dawns
So the New Year does come
A fresh way to work
With hope our race we'll run

We hope the old year was a blessing
In all you did do
In everything you were successful
Your actions were true

The New Year is your opportunity
To work for your end
So go forward and make it so
Your future to begin

We hope that in the coming year
You will successful be
As in every new day
A better life you will see

THE HOPES

The hopes in the past
Were born of where we were
A time and a place long ago
When all possibilities seemed to stir

The hopes for today
Are what we now seek
That we may do the better
In every day, in every week

The New Year is like a new day
When we can begin much again
Make plans to succeed
Our race in life to win

So we wish you the very best
In all you say and do
That in the New Year
Much you hold will come true

LIFE IS A TRIP

Life is a trip
The New Year is a door
To the future
Where life will be more

Through the door we must go
Into the unknown
The land of opportunities
The world where dreams are sown

The future will be bright
The opportunities good
What we do with them
Is our choice, if we could

So prepare for the best
The new world awaits you
To be what you can be
So good and so true

YEAR IN, YEAR OUT

Year in, year out
Time goes slowly by
But at this time of year
The New Year draws nigh

Greet friends and family
Gather round and eat
To have so many here
Is really quite a treat

It is nice to have
The ones about we care
To come to see us
To be there

So now we celebrate
With love and good cheer
For it is the time we meet
To wish you a Happy New Year!

A NEW DAY DAWNS

A new day dawns
A New Year does come
A fresh start in life
Our race we'll run

Bless the old year
With all you did do
In everything you were successful
Your actions were true

Work the work of the New Year
Work as only you can do
Live life to the fullest
To make your wishes come true

In this New Year
May you successful be
As in every new day
A better life you will see

ANOTHER YEAR

Another year has come and gone
With battles fought and victories won
We are better for what we've done
But time slips by and is gone

We can revel this time of year
In the good that has come our way
And look forward to the New Year
Where we will live, come what may

So celebrate this time of year
The future is ours to behold
That we may follow our star
Before the year gets old

We wish the best for you
For all the good things you do
May you be the best you can be
And your motives be true

YEAR OF LOVE

The year began with promise
We did not know what it would bring
Whether we would have the bad
Or it would make our spirit sing

The future we cannot know
It is clouded in the mist of time
But it is a slate upon which is written
With the glory of the eternal prime

If we are good and kind
If we make the future our own
We find that when it arrives
We will reap what we have sown

So we should know what to do
To give what is good and kind and true
And in the eternal book of life
We will have whatever we did do

ROAD OF LIFE

The road of life is a long road
Where we have a blessed choice
In this holiday season
For good we can rejoice

For the hand of the Almighty
From long past, from our birth
That we may live and prosper
For the good things that come to the earth

So let us to the less fortunate remember
When as we go to the season of light
That but for the grace of God go I
May we be as we should in Heaven's sight

There are many roads we travel
Through this world as we go
So let us be as we should
Blessings we may know

TO ALL WE WISH

To all we wish a happy holiday
To your kind and kin
May you celebrate
We wish a good New Year to begin

For in this world of toil and sin
There is much we cannot know
But to give to others good
As through the year we go

So enjoy life as it comes
The bad and the good
It is our troubles
That makes us as we should

So have a holy season
From the heavens above
Let us all know the truth
Of fellowship and of love

CHRISTMAS IS THE TIME OF YEAR

Christmas is the time of year
For love, joy and good cheer
It is the beginning and the end
Of the New Year that we will spend

But when you look
At the presents under the tree
Please try to remember
The One given to us so free

He came in love
To show us the Way
To live with each other
What we should do and say

When I see the Christmas tree
The presents for me
I will try to remember
The One who helped set me free

THE END OF THE WORLD

The end of the world is at hand
So it seems each day
When it comes
There will be no other way

But in this season of joy
Let nothing so despair
For when the New Year comes
We will all be there

Don't believe the naysayer
For always they are there
Always they are wrong
Their challenges are not fair

So live in the New Year
Let nothing you annoy
But keep the faith
In this season of joy

Believe in the future
Live life as the good doth call
Sit beside the road
And be a friend to all

WHEN IN THE COURSE

When in the course of human events
The year passes from one to another
We enter the New Year with fear and hope
That the new will serve us better

Our hope is in the future
The past we already know
For deeds both bad and good
Often we reap better than we sow

But we can work for the best
Never let the present rest
That we will be as we are
May we find that we are blessed

So when comes the New Year
May all your hopes come true
That by the by and by your try
You will have the best that's new

GIVE THANKS

Give thanks unto the Lord
Give thanks for all we have
For those who the Lord has blessed
Life and love He does give

To give Him thanks is His due
It is what we must
For unto the Holy God
We give our total trust

We may not know why we should give thanks
For all that we have
But consider that it is
What we receive, what we can give

So as we celebrate
With family and friend
Let us truly know that God
Is with us till the end

WHO IS GOD?

Who is God?
What is His name?
His name is YAHWEH
From age to age the same

By His Holy Love
He sent His Son to earth
So that all who believe
Can have the Spiritual Birth

Today in the world He works
Through the Holy Spirit's desire
That all may know His comfort
This gives the Church His power

These three are one
In purpose, in love, in power
Their eternal will for mankind
Is God's eternal desire

MEASURING TIME

We measure time by the year
So much yet to eternally be
We grow in wisdom and truth
To many things yet to see

The year has passed and is gone
For many things that are good and true
We have strived to do our best
But so much yet to do

The year is for us a hope
That it will prosper us
Be for us a way to live
Not be an eternal bust

We will work together
Our race of life to run
That by the by
We will become truly one

THERE IS ONE WAY

There is one Way
And only one
The Way to Heaven
The Way our eternal life begun

We can find the Way
By what God has done
It is the Holy One
It is God's Holy Son

Begotten by God
Lived among men
Has seen us from the first
Will see us till the end

Follow the Way
The Way to a Holy Life
All other ways of life
Will lead to eternal strife

We can know the Way
The only Way given among men
By which we must be saved
Eternal life to begin

That is this Way
The Way given by God
It is to follow His Son
Ere we're beneath the sod

THE SEARCH

We search for what we do not know
For the way we should live
We find the path of life
When we learn to give

Our guide was given
By the Holy Life
When God sent His only Son
To guide us from eternal strife

It was so long ago
He taught us how
To live for God above
In the past and in the now

Let us so bless the Lord above
For His Holy love
That we may be forever blessed
By the life given from above

There is no other way
To know God's Holy Will
But to follow in the Holy Way
That we may love all, not kill

To aid those who do not have
The means to make the day
But must beg from us
The Lord asks us to pay

So praise the Lord above
That we may find the Way
To show His Holy Will
And mean it when a blessing we say

God expects us to keep His Will
Expects us to know His Way
To look to those who are with us
He will walk with us today

THE SPECIAL DAY

Upon the special day
Was born the hope of mankind
So that by His Life and by His Word
It is Heaven we may find

He came and taught and lived
Taught us how to give
How to be born of the Spirit
How the Children of God must live

Lived so long ago
In the reckoning of men
But came, the revolution to give
The new age to begin

Now we live in His shadow
In what He lived and taught
So that we may treat others in love
To live as we ought

THE DAYS GROW SHORT

The days grow short
Jack Frost on the windows
Snow across the trails
Now it is almost Christmas

We have a warm house
With family and friends
Celebrate this time of year
Soon New Year begins

Love those who are with us
To help us celebrate
Christmas is coming
Almost can't wait

The joy in Christmas
Is to give to those we love
To see their eyes sparkle
Like the stars above

WINTER GOLF

Golf is a game played
When the sun does shine
When the ground is covered with snow
White golf balls are hard to find

So what to do in days so drear
When we must answer the call
There is a solution so clear
Use balls that are dark, that's all

You swing a miss in summer
A little dirt you pick up
Miss the ball in winter
Snow in the face is what you get

Then we look for the ball
If we hit out it of bounds
It may be beneath the snow
It will be hidden, not found

Then we try to find the green
Where is the hole we seek
In the summer it is right there
Now buried in the white streak

When at last we find the green
If we have a hole-in-one
We are all alone
If we tell, who thinks we're done

We can boast
We can ask others to understand
But don't expect them to believe
It is a far-fetched plan

HOME WITH FRIENDS

When the winter wind blows
There is no place to go
A time to stay home with your own
A good time we may know

We have so much to talk about
So much now there is time
In summer we were so busy, going out
This is what is mine

There was me and there was you
Now there is us
That we can know each other
Now we can have a deeper trust

May this season be one of love
May we truly understand
That the more we are one
The stronger we stand

CHRISTMAS HOLIDAY

The holiday of Christmas
Is the day of song and joy
To celebrate with family and friends
For every girl and boy

Presents under the tree
Are there for each one
That on Christmas morning
Our joy has just begun

We think of Santa and good cheer
It is with us each day
Follow the day of living
Good tidings we say

So love and good cheer
May be with us in every way
And go in and out with us
Throughout every day

THE DAYS OF CHRISTMAS

The days of Christmas
When we celebrate
Give for the love of others
To those who cannot wait

We should love like God
For the children of men
Treat them with compassion
A new day to begin

Can we know the Way
That God would have us walk
Truly do the best
Not just talk the talk

Guilty we should not be
For we must love God's stand
Taught by His Holy Word
Who was and is the Son of Man

So love all this world
So live as we know we should
Walk the Holy Path
Follow His Holy Word

ABOUT THE AUTHOR

The author has been a Christian and church member for many years. In the past 20 years, inspired by his mother's experience as a poet, he has written poems on many subjects, some of which are included in this work.

Richard was born in Bartow, Florida. He has been married for 50 years to his sweetheart, who is an accomplished artist. They have 2 children and 3 grandchildren.

www.ingramcontent.com/pod-product-compliance
Lightning Source LLC
Chambersburg PA
CBHW032135040426
42449CB00005B/256